Running For Your Life!

A devotional for women who run slow, walk fast or jog with reckless abandon

---

Richelle Clark

Strawberry Sky Inc.

For Leona Bell, who showed me how
to run with God!

A note from the author: This
devotional began when my friend
Fatima asked me to write a monthly
devotional for women at our church,
called Meeting Point. Some of these
devotionals were originally sent as e-
mails to the women of Riverside
International Church in Lisbon,
Portugal and others were written
exclusively for this devotional. I hope
that you enjoy them all!

Dear sisters,

Take this devotional with you as you run or walk. It should fit in your pocket or fanny pack. When you need rest, or encouragement, pull it out and read a page or two. Also, jot down some of your own thoughts and prayers in this book. I hope this devotional can be a blessing to you.

With Love,

    Richelle

Library of Congress Control Number:
2011937046

Scripture quoted from this book comes from the Living Bible, King James and NIV versions of the Bible.

Strawberry Sky Inc. publishes devotionals, studies and books to help you along your spiritual journey. For more information on upcoming books, please write us at
strawberryskyinc@yahoo.com

Contents:

Part I.

The benefits of running for your life

Running for Your Life!

A while back I ran the Portugal Half Marathon. It wasn't pretty or fast, but I finished.

At the start of the race, all of the participants sped down the Vasco De Gama Bridge in Lisbon. I ran to the bathroom. I had a sudden urge to pee. When I was done, I walked out of the portable toilet only to be stuck in a wave or walkers, baby strollers and joggers who were participating in a simultaneous mini marathon.

I was so far behind the marathon runners that it was a mental struggle. I couldn't see the correct signs. I made a wrong turn, went up a steep hill and wound up on the highway.

Eek!

Then, I had to double back, find a marathon official and find the "real" marathon course. I was embarrassed, but I kept going. Then, when I started setting a good pace, a transit cop drove up next to me, to see if I was able to finish the race. I was nearly in last place.

"You know you have to run all the way down and then come all the way back," the official told me in Portuguese.

"Yes, I am good," I told him.

"Are you sure?"

"Yes, I am good, "I told him.

I don't think he believed me because he kept riding beside me in his motorcycle. Then, from the other side of the street, a group of runners coming back toward the finish line appeared and some of them were my friends. I will not forget what they yelled from across the street:

"Richelle, don't let him intimidate you. Keep running."

"Força," other runners yelled back at me in Portuguese, as I plodded along the trail.

I kept going. The cop sped away.

It took me nearly two hours to make it to the half-way point. I began praying even harder now. As I was making my way, I realized something that changed everything. This was not just a half marathon -- this was an allegory for my life!

Boy have I gotten lost a lot in this life. I have had others try to talk me out of what I believe. I even felt like giving up a time or two, but I kept on going. Sometimes I didn't feel like I was good enough, but I made my way through, asking God to direct my path.

I finished the half marathon. My friends who gave me words of encouragement were waiting for me at the finish line.

When I look back at that experience,   I am reminded of the Apostle Paul, who tells us to "run your race to win."

To win the contest you must deny yourselves many things that would keep you from doing your best. An athlete goes to all this trouble just to win a blue ribbon or a silver cup, but we do it for a heavenly reward that never disappears (Living Bible I Corinthians 9:24-25).

Paul also tells us in the book of Hebrews that we should run with patience this life that God has given us. So, dear sisters, continue to run the marathon of life! Do not let others talk you out of your important work, ministry or beliefs.

Our goal is not to beat someone else's record, or to run a pretty looking race, but to finish and win the prize that awaits us -- heaven. So please, please, keep running for your life!

Richelle

The Strength of God – His Fortifications Outlast Castles

In the mornings, I like to run or walk on the boardwalk along the Lisbon Coast from the tiny city of Sao Joao do Estoril to the more touristy Cascais. And along my journey, I like to breathe in the fresh ocean air, feel the warm sun on my arms and I especially like watching the families and small children who seem so thrilled to be on the beach.

The children are so happy to be splashing in the water or building sand castles. Their parents seem a bit worn out though, from continually telling their children to take care of the waves or not to go to deep in the water. But the children are ignorant of their parents stress, always believing that if they get into trouble, their strong parents would help them.

I something think we are the same way.

As I walk, I can´t help but notice the strong and imposing forts and castle-like structures that dot along the coast. They are magnificently strong, beautiful and weathered. When I see them, I am reminded of Psalm 31.

To paraphrase part of the psalm, it says that in times of trouble, we can call out to God to be our rock and refuge because he is a strong fortress to save us.

"Since you are my rock and my fortress, for the sake of your name lead and guide me. Free me from the trap that is set for me, for you are my refuge," Psalm 31:3-4 (NIV).

So I know that while I am running on the beach, or running to do the next thing on my list, that God is also leading me and guiding me in my life and I know for sure that he is my refuge, he is my fortress and he delights in me following Him.

To him, I am like the squealing children playing on the beach, trusting their parent to care for them if they need any help.

May we continue to follow Him and remember that he is a great refuge not only in times of trouble, but in times of joy!

Songs of God

I love church music. Sometimes I used to visit churches just to hear their choirs. It was as if the music touched my soul.

When I was a young Christian, I didn't quite understand all of what I read in the Bible -- whether it was the King James' version or NIV. At times I thought the Bible was like calculus or physics and I was barely competent in arithmetic and science. I felt a bit embarrassed and not sure who to talk to about it.

I talked with my pastor. I kept reading God's word. And when I felt a bit overwhelmed or lost, it always seemed as if the church choir would find a song that would speak to my heart and give me clarity on His word.

As I continued to grow in Christ, I learned about beautiful songs in the Bible – the Psalms. These are some of the sweetest songs ever written to praise God. Many of them were written by King David, who sure did know how to praise God.

I especially love Psalm 138, entitled God Answered My Prayer. In times of trouble, I recite this Psalm because it offers me comfort and it reassures me that God is here and that he will answer my prayers.

In Psalm 138, the Psalmist writes: "*When I called, you answered me. You made me bold and stouthearted* (NIV, verse 3)."

He also goes on to say: "*Though I walk in the midst of trouble, you preserve my life. You stretch out your hand against the anger of my foes, with your right hand, you save me* (verse 7)."

In addition to strengthening me, I have learned that I can read and sing the Psalms when I want to rest comfortably with God or just praise Him. I don't have to reach for these songs when I am feeling low, but I can also recite them in joy and triumph! This week, may we continue celebrating God in thought, prayer and music … and in his sweet Psalms.

Part II

Fruits of the Spirit – to Give Us Nourishment

But the fruit of the Spirit is love, joy, peace, longsuffering, gentleness, goodness, faith, meekness, temperance: against such there is no law. Galatians 5:22-23. (King James version)

Love is What God Does and Who He is

But the fruit of the Spirit is love, joy, peace, longsuffering, gentleness, goodness, faith, meekness, temperance: against such there is no law. Galatians 5:22-23. (King James)

When I was born, my mother was just 18 years old. She and my father did not marry. She asked her big sister to take me before I was born. Her sister was in her late 20s, had one son and a husband. My aunt could not have any more children, and so, she welcomed me into her family.

I was a needy kid, in part because I feared being abandoned by my new parents. I thought there was something wrong with me because my birth parents did not keep me. My Aunt seemed to carry this burden too, but she loved and encouraged me –telling me that I could do or be anything in this life. She didn´t want me to use my issues with abandonment as an excuse for mediocrity or failure.

However, my abandonment issues seemed to increase when my uncle and aunt split. A few years later he died from cancer and I was devastated. I had formed a great bond with my uncle, who was my "daddy" and who showed me unconditional love.

My birth mother went on to have other children and there were parts of me that wished she would come back for me. I wanted this mythical "perfect mommy," to return and claim me. Now when I look back on this, I see how ungrateful I was because I had my aunt who cared for and loved me. I was too busy stewing in pain and misery instead of embracing the life and opportunities that God had given me. Other children in similar circumstances were not as fortunate as I – I realize this now.

But issues of my past and abandonment would continue to haunt me, even when I was married and pregnant with my daughter. I will discuss this later.

I am grateful for the love and care that I received growing up. My aunt loved me and helped inspire me to do my best. She later adopted me and gave me her name. She had become the mommy that I needed and had hoped for. It was a blessing that God put her into my life to raise me.

In time, I was able to focus on something other than my pain. I looked to school; I had dreams of what I might be able to accomplish in life. I wanted to be a writer. I wanted to travel the world. I have been able to do those things. I know that two things made all of those things possible: My aunt, who became my mother and main cheerleader; and a group of wiry missionaries who came walking down my inner-city neighborhood to tell me and my friends about Jesus. I was so excited about this good news! God would be with me always!

But I must admit. I have continued to struggle with issues of abandonment and doubting people's love for me – especially during trials.

My husband and I have also struggled with fertility issues, which seemed to highlight my abandonment issues all the more. To make a long story short, when I was pregnant with my daughter, I suffered all manner of problems and I felt God had abandoned me.

Throughout the complications I experienced during my pregnancy, I was praying and reading the Bible ... and praying even more. People who I didn't know were praying for us. I was hospitalized three times. I was on bed rest. I took to my bed with great fervor and prayers and kept busy writing a book and started two others. A few months later, my daughter was born, and it was such a joy to see and meet her.

For years, I had secretly accused God of abandoning me during that time. I did the same thing as a child when I acted up because my mother gave me up and did not return to claim me as I thought she should have.

It started to seem as if God left me just when I needed him most. Why didn't he stop the bleeding, the pain and the complications? Why didn't he give me a stress free pregnancy? Why did I feel so alone during those dark times? Why did it feel like God was some other place except for with me? Was I to blame for this? Nothing made sense.

I often read Psalm 138 – God answered my prayer. One part goes: in the day when I cried you answered me and strengthened me with strength in my soul. Another part goes: thou I walk in the midst of trouble, thou wilt revive me and strengthen me with strength in my soul.

I hadn't felt God had really done these things when I was pregnant. Was I wrong to assume my heavenly father did not care about His creation?

Yes. And I was even starting to get on my own nerves!

Since my daughter's birth, I know better. I have had more miscarriages. It is unlikely that I will ever give birth to another child. I see that God did indeed answer my prayers for a child and that he had never abandoned me. He gave me the strength I needed to endure so that I could give birth to my daughter.

God is an awesome God. He heard Hannah's cries for a child and gave her Samuel, a holy man to be used for God's purpose (see the books of Samuel in the Old Testament). And then she gave her son away to fulfill a promise she made to God!

I am no Hannah! But somehow, God took pity on me and all of my ungratefulness and gave me a child. I know that many other women have prayed and been faithful and they did not have children. I know many more women suffer from heartache from miscarriages and feel no relief – not even with constant prayers. I do not know why this is the case, but God knows all. He loves these women and he will never abandon them either. I know this because he did not abandon me.

But this is what I know: God answers all of our prayers – not always the way we want him to.

God gave me the parents I needed to survive and thrive. I am fortunate to have two mothers who love and encourage me. I am close to both my birth mother and adoptive mother. My daughter has two grandmothers to spoil her! God also made sure that I became a Christian just when I needed him most – as a young child experiencing loss.

One day, I am sure, when I am older, a doctor will be able tell me what specific kinds of problems I had with fertility and I am sure they will wonder how I was ever able to have any child at all. I believe this. But all I could tell them or anyone else is that God is the reason I have a child. He is the reason I am alive and made it out of the inner city when smarter and more gifted youth did not. He heard my cries, my pleas and even through my constant begging, he blessed me – even though he knew that I would turn around and accuse him of abandoning me, of not really loving me.

 I am ashamed of how I behaved and all the more grateful that God is good, holy, and full of forgiveness for sinners like me.

I know that God loves me. I know that I am blessed and I hope to never doubt the love and protection my God has offered me and my family.

This week dear sisters, remember how much God loves you. I implore you to share your struggles with each other not to wallow in self-pity, but to teach others that they too can overcome heartache and disappointment.

I also hope that your stories will show others God´s mercy and love.

I am sharing this personal story with you because I hope that you can avoid my mistakes of thinking that God abandons his children. Life will not be without disappointment, but there will be love, and joy and triumph when you walk on His path. But more importantly, there will be God.

Praise be to God!

Finding Joy is Easier than Finding My Keys!

One day I was in a hurry to meet a friend at a nearby cafe. But I could not find my house keys to lock the door. I then went into panic mode: I searched each floor of the house. I ran upstairs and looked around. I ran downstairs and attempted to retrace my steps. I searched my purse. I even checked the side door to see if I left the keys in the lock. I was batting zero!

My frustration grew. When I was about to give up, I threw up my hands. When they came down, I heard a jingle.

"Oh," I thought. "My keys are in my pocket."

Boy did I feel dumb! My keys were with me all along!

My days can be a lot like my empty search for my keys. I can be busy doing work that I feel is important and something comes along and steals my joy. It could be an accident, a harsh word, disappointment or my own struggle with perfectionism and suddenly I feel like a victim. My joy was stolen and I am at a lost as to what to do to get it back.

But when I feel this way, I can remember the Apostle Paul who seemed to have joy in all circumstances. It did not matter if he was beaten, imprisoned or spreading the good news in jail, he did not give up hope. He was filled with joy.

I must admit that I have had more joyless days than I care to admit. But God has left me a wonderful life map called the Bible to help me find my way out of the abyss. I can remember Psalm 16 when I feel down. In this beautiful poem of praise, the psalmist asks God to direct his life's path:

"You make known to me the path of life; you will fill me with joy in your presence, with eternal pleasures at your hand. (NIV Psalm 16: 11)

So, God has already filled us with the joy of his presence! We only need to tap into it, to remind ourselves of this wonderful gift.

We can also feel comfort in reading Psalm 30, a prayer of deliverance. I pay special attention to verses 4 and 5 (Living Bible translation):

"Oh sing to him you saints of his; give thanks to his holy name. His anger lasts a moment; his favor lasts for life! Weeping and may go on all night, but in the morning there is joy."

As we focus our thoughts on joy – the fruit of the spirit – may we remember that in our darkest times that we have hope and we have assurance that joy comes in the morning and that joy in the Lord is with us always!

Peace

Often times, it seems as if peace eludes me. I get so busy with life that I forget to take time to experience the gift of peace.

In the Bible, God has called for us to "Live in Peace." It is ours, ready for us. We have to reach out for it and take it – the same way we would take a second helping of food!

This week, may we seek peace and find it not because we are good hunters, but because God has made it ready and available to us.

May we set aside quiet time to talk to God, read the books 1Corinthians and 2Corinthians and meditate on His word!

Patience and Brownie Cake

My daughter Abby loves dessert. In fact, she sometimes only eats her dinner just to have the sweet treat that follows. Her favorites are chocolate ice cream or a special brownie cake topped with nuts and chocolate chips.

I have learned a lot about myself and my faith walk as I raise my daughter. It is as if new things are revealed to me each day -- like how wanting dessert can teach us all about patience.

I have noticed that during dinner Abby sometimes rushes through her meal. And after taking her last bite, she pushes her plate away from her and declares, "all done."

"Now, can I have dessert?" she asks.

"No Abby," I tell her. "You must wait until mommy and daddy finish eating."

"Aww,"she says, followed by "OK."

Just as my husband and I finish our meal, Abby looks at us, full of excitement and I know what is coming next:

"OK, now can I have my dessert?"

"Yes, but you have to wait for mommy to get the dessert,"

"Awww, she declares."

She hasn´t quite mastered patience. She doesn´t like to wait for something good, something sweet. She wants it now and without delay. Unfortunately, her mommy is a lot like that, especially in her walk with God.

There have been many times that I have acted as Abby, but instead of wanting dessert, I wanted God to immediately fix a problem or give me something that I requested from him. I ask him for something and when the response is wait, my response is "Awww."

What´s worse is that sometimes I might keep asking him in the hopes that it will speed up his reply. But unfortunately it doesn´t necessarily work that way. In our Christian walk, we cannot always have dessert. We have to have patience and wait on God to give us a full meal, sometimes without the dessert we crave.

Sometimes, it seems as if my daughter has learned this lesson, as I still struggle with it.

When she finally gets dessert, she is grateful, happy and smacks her lips. Every now and then I get a "You´re the best mommy ever." Then within a few moments I hear her scraping the bottom of the bowl or licking brownie off her fingers.

Dear sisters, may we also find our patience, relying on God to provide all of our needs. And when he answers our prayers, may we savor the sweet dessert given to us by our Lord and Savior. I am sure that God doesn´t mind if we scrape our bowls too, or even give him shouts of praise.

Riding the Bus to Kindness

When I was a young girl, my mother decided to teach me how to ride the public bus system in my native Philadelphia. We boarded the bus, got bus transfers and got off the bus so she could go to the bank and purchase a few items.

I do not remember where she sent me, but I was to go to another store then get on the bus to return home. My mom said she would hop on that same bus at the next stop. I do not know what happened, but I got on the bus headed in the opposite direction.

When I realized my error, I was paralyzed with fear. I felt that I would never get home.

The bus went to the end of the line -- another city -- and the driver told me that I had to get off. I ran to the nearest phone and called my mother collect on the pay phone. She managed to hear my story through sobs.

My mom told me to explain my situation to the bus driver in the hopes he would let me ride the bus for free. You see, I had no money. And my mom could not come get me. I was miles away from home. But I was too frightened to approach the bus driver. Two elderly ladies saw me crying and asked me what was going on.

I explained to them that I had gotten on the wrong bus. I was frightened, still crying and I didn´t know what to do. They were very kind and calmed me down. Then one of the women, reached inside of her pocketbook, found her tiny change purse and carefully counted out the 45 cents I needed to ride the bus back home.

I was so happy.

"I was going home! I was going home!" I thought to myself.

In my happiness, I forgot to properly thank the woman. The other lady, reminded me of my manners. She told me that her friend did not have much money and that she was doing me a great kindness. I thanked them both for their help.

I boarded the bus, took a deep breath and began my journey home. When I reached my stop, I got off of the bus and just about ran home. I was so happy to see my street, my house, my mom.

For a moment, when I was lost, my home seemed so far from me and my mother unreachable. Yet a stranger, who I did not know, was very kind to me, a scared young girl.

When I look back on this event, I can now see how Jesus also shows us a similar form of kindness. We were once lost with no hope of getting to our real home, but Jesus reached into his heart and told us about our Heavenly Father and showed us that by believing in him, we could reach our true home. So, in a way, our very own salvation begins with an act of kindess.

Dear sisters, may we remember while on our life journey, that kindness is more than just a descriptive word, or way to help a scared kid ride the bus, but an act that can forever change our physical and spiritual destinations.

Goodness

When I was young, I remember some church folk saying that only God is good. But as an older Christian, I understand that we can follow in His footsteps, imitating Him and showing goodness when life's trials call us up and want to visit.

Sometimes it is hard for us to display such "moral excellence" even when we know it is expected. We can sometimes fall prey to our humanness and forget about this quiet little fruit of the spirit – especially since it is near the bottom. But it is nonetheless, a calling for all of us.

I remember a time when I was young and moral excellence was a challenge I wasn't sure I wanted to meet. I can now look back on that situation and see not only my mother's hand literally whacking my bottom, but also the hand of God in molding me to be a better person.

When I was in elementary school, I went to visit my cousin Rhonda. She lived about a half a mile from my house and I walked to get there. When I arrived, I was a bit bored and decided I would sneak off to visit another cousin – Adrian-- who lived about two blocks away. When I arrived at Adrian's house I called my mother and told her I was at Rhonda's house.

My mom, knowing me all too well, knew that something wasn't quite right and called Rhonda's house to check on me. It was then that she learned that I was not there, but in fact, visiting another cousin.

After playing and talking with Adrian, I walked home –thinking nothing of my telephone deception. I played and talked with my cousin and behaved myself. But when I strutted home, I was met with a spanking!?!

Yup.

I lied to my mother about where I was. I behaved badly. You see, my mother expected moral excellence of me – even though I was in elementary school. Had I told her the truth of where I was, I would not have gotten a spanking. But she spanked me to discourage me from lying and being deceptive. Because I did not have a high tolerance for pain (spankings), I immediately knew that I had to do better.

As adults, our heavenly father calls all of us to an even higher standard of goodness. He knows that we are not perfect, and can make mistakes. And from time to time, if we do not walk in the goodness that we are called to, we may feel as if we are getting spanked.

It is at this point of the message that I tell you how grateful I am for grace – undeserved forgiveness -- and even more grateful for the example of Jesus who literally was all of the fruits of the spirit.

May we think about all of the fruits of the spirit, especially goodness, which seems to have such a high bar, then, we should reach for some grace and continue our faith walk, showing goodness where and when we can.

Faithfulness

When I think of faithfulness, I am reminded of my grandmother Leona Bell Whitney.

She lived to be in her late 80s and her faithfulness seemed to increase with age. She started every day with a prayer. This prayer began when she carefully got on her knees to talk with her Savior. She also read devotionals and sang spirituals while doing housework.

As an adult nearing middle age, I have been guilty of lazy prayers sometimes uttered as I am about to go to sleep. I do not get on my knees to pray as my grandmother. Nor do I always spend quiet time with God every day as I should. My grandmother did this, and even with poor eyesight, she still read her Bible regularly. Leona Bell, who we all called Mom, was a spiritual mentor of sorts. She showed me the importance of continuing my journey with God.

My grandmother did not have an easy life – not too many people of her generation did. She worked as a domestic to put food on the table, raised five children and encouraged them all in their faith walk. She outlived two of her husbands. By default, she became the spiritual head of our family and she took that job seriously.

She went to church every week, prayed often and was quick to tell us to forgive and to take care about how we spoke to each other. She gave unselfishly and was a surrogate mother and grandmother to many.

Before she became ill with heart problems, you could always find her in the kitchen, singing the songs of God and cooking up something tasty. I can still remember her singing old hymns while making a batch of her sweet rolls. Yum!

When she wasn´t cooking for her family, she was praying for them. She believed that God would answer her prayers and that her Savior would make a way for us. She was right.

I believe that some of the blessings God has bestowed upon me and my siblings are the direct result of the prayers Leona Bell uttered for her family. My grandmother showed me how to love God and to serve him.

My grandmother is no longer here, but her lessons remain. We can all be prayer warriors for our families and loved ones. We can commit to quiet time with God and being careful to record the blessing so that we can see how much He has blessed us. Our spiritual journey is not a contest – there is no first or second place. However, we will all have room on the winner´s podium and a place in heaven. That is reward enough.

You might also have a family member who was strong in their faith. Remember their great lessons of faith, love and leadership. Think of them often, like I think of my grandmother. Take from their lives what you can and improve your own. See them as great coaches who inspire you.

Leona Bell was my coach – she is the one who really taught me how to run with God.

Gentleness

Have you watched those nature television shows when a ferocious lioness is tracking down, then sinking her teeth into some gazelle or other type of fluffy animal?

The lioness displays such ferocity and you do not want to cross her path – especially when she is hungry.

But if you watch that same program, you will see the lioness giving her newborn cubs a bath with her tongue. She is careful and displays gentleness as she licks and paws her little ones. She also displays great patience as they try to feed (Anyone who has ever breast fed their infant will appreciate the words patience and gentleness!).

It might be hard to believe that the same animal can be both gentle and ferocious. Ferocious because she needs the meat from the animal to produce milk to feed her cubs and gentle when caring for those same babies.

We must also display the same kind of attributes in our life. We must be ferocious in protecting our family from harm, always trusting in our Savior, and gentle in protecting those we love and care for.

The lioness can teach us much about life!

Self-control: A Lesson for Mommy

When my daughter was born, she didn´t know much about self-control.

I think I also had a lot to learn.

When she was hungry, she cried. When her diaper was wet she complained in her special baby language. And when she wanted attention, she let me know with cries or baby babble that she wanted me to pick her up and play with her. She did not care to wait or to control herself – this was foreign to her. She was depending on her earthly mother to give her the things she needed. This is normal for a baby.

But there were times that she behaved out of control – even when she knew she should not. When she was a toddler and didn´t get what she wanted, she threw fits. A few times she got down on the grocery store floor and screamed. It was an Oscar-worthy performance because I nearly cried too!

This is the point where my new lesson in self-control began. I had to display self-control and not spank her little bottom in anger!

Eventually, I learned a new kind of self-control. I could walk away from her when she fell out on the floor and screamed.

And finally we both learned that if she was naughty she could get a smack on the bottom and be placed on time out.

Just like my daughter, we must learn about self-control, but it is a process that never seems to end.

It is one of those fruits of the spirit that we all know about but sometimes are not as enthusiastic about embracing for fear of appearing weak in front of others.

We learn that in life, we must behave a certain way. When we are hungry and the waiter is taking his time putting in our order, we cannot cry and demand to eat right now. And when we want a raise from our boss, we cannot sit on the office floor and kick and scream until we get what we want – although I have secretly wanted to throw a fit or two at work.

Nor can we stomp our feet when we are left to clean up our own messes, when we perceive we are without heavenly help.

It is the same with our spiritual walk and our relationship with God.

We may feel at times that we are failing at self-control and our Christian walk. But we must realize that Christ was a living example for us in self-control.

He displayed self-control, seeming to say what needed to be said in a controlled manner. He even loved those who displayed little self-control.

With hard work, we can mirror him. We can learn that our struggles are not so much about our will, but God´s will and that we can surrender all to our heavenly father.

While this may not immediately end or resolve our issues with control, it is a beginning. It is a process that may take one week or 10 years, but if we are faithful, we will get to the other side, meaning a victory in Christ Jesus!

Part III.

More Devotionals

Skinny Legs and All

When I was a young girl, I was very self-conscious about my legs. Who am I kidding? Until recently, I felt a sense of shame about my legs because I have thin calf legs and ankles.

I have been teased by relatives and friends a time or two. I have been called chicken legs and have been lambasted for having an athletic build of "straight up and down." I secretly hoped that puberty would make my legs shapelier.

But after puberty, some parts of me grew out, but my legs stayed thin. And as I reached adulthood, I didn´t know what it was like to have hips or big legs. However, I thought that it was a sign of beauty.

I hardly ever wore shorts as a youth and definitely not as an adult. I did not wear short skirts or walking shorts. In the 1980s I tried to compensate for my skinny legs by wearing leg warmers. In the 1990s I wore boots that came up to my knees. And afterwards, I just wore pants or long skirts and dresses because I didn´t want to show my legs.

Even though I exercised regularly, I only saw problems with my figure: My belly was too big because I did not have a six pack, my breasts were too small, my legs were too thin, and my toes too ugly. The list goes on.

I was so concerned with my outer beauty and what I wanted to change that it made me sad and self-conscious. I was behaving terribly. I had forgotten the words of God – that we should trust in him rather than our beauty. In the book of Proverbs God cautions that beauty does not last ... but a woman who fears the Lord shall be praised (NIV paraphrase).

Psalm 139 also reminds us that we are "fearfully and wonderfully made" and that our bodies were knitted by you, oh God, in our mothers´ wombs.

Even though I knew all of these things and I have a loving husband who loves all of me, I still felt shame about my body. I wanted what I perceived as better.

Then something marvelous happened.

One day I decided in all of my crazy that I would train to run a half marathon. I had watched a few marathons on television and saw that some of the runners were built like me -- I mean they had thin legs too. In fact, the runners had all kinds of body shapes and legs.

So I ran that half marathon. When I was done, I started to gradually change how I saw inner and outer beauty. For the first time, I saw my own legs as beautiful and strong, not because they were shapely or perfect, but because they got me to the finish line.

My legs have carried my daughter up the stairs when she was tired and chased after her in play.

I have used my legs to walk on the boardwalk or run on the sand. I have hiked mountains (in high heels!) and traveled the world … on these legs.

Now, I do not feel shame about my legs – just gratefulness.

So, did some magic transformation happen after running the marathon? Nope. My legs are still thin, but I can now wear shorts on the beach with my daughter. I do not hold onto shame about the shape and size of my legs. They are strong and powerful just the way they are. I will never be Tina Turner, but I can confidently embrace all of me, skinny legs and all.

Dear sisters, as we begin our physical and spiritual journey to run, walk or get into shape. May we see our bodies, not as imperfect or missing something, but a great work created by God. May we embrace our bodies, knowing that we too, were fearfully and wonderfully fashioned by Him, who is working to shape up all of us, from the inside out!

Running From Your Past

The Apostle Paul tells us a lot about the person he was before he knew Christ. He also talks of the person he became thanks to Jesus.

Paul seemed to have no problem facing his past and getting about the business of doing God´s work of spreading the good news.

I have not been so fortunate. In fact, there are days that I wish that I could forget parts of the past – or better yet have other people forget about my past too.

I have struggled for years with the effects of being molested. The abuse came mostly from other children, who probably didn´t quite understand it all themselves. We just knew that it was wrong.

I struggled with depression about this part of my past, feeling dirty and a great disappointment to God. This issue was magnified because I was not being raised by my birth parents, and I guess I didn´t think I was worthy of that. I even wondered what was wrong with me that these things had happened.

I struggled with teenage awkwardness, probably more than most, because of my other burdens.

As a result, I closed myself off from people, from relationships and just retreated to nice daydreams and fantasies, where I thought I would be safe.

I went to school, I worked, I interacted, but tried not to form close bonds with most people. Everything was just on the surface – a manner in which I thought would protect me from pain.

But it turns out, not only did it not free me from pain, but I missed out a lot of life because I was spending so much time with a fake reality.

And I realized, that if I could face my past, my mistakes, my burdens, that I could live a much fuller life, if I was brave enough to do so.

On the days that I feel sorry for myself, I am reminded of the Apostle Paul, who ran a good race for God. He was not burdened by his past, but he did accept responsibility for what he did and what happened in his old life and new one.

You see, before Paul became a Christian, he actually persecuted Christians. Yet, God saved him and made him an important part of His ministry.

God can purify our hearts and our bodies. He can help us to face our past, but remove the shame and hurt associated with past mistakes and bad things that happened to us. He can free us from the past so that we can better live in the present.

So, yes, while there are times I still want to outrun my past, I also know that I cannot. It will always be with me. But here is the good news: Jesus is always with me too! Because of God, the past does not control me and tell me to run away from people and situations, to hide. I am not my past, but it is a part of me. And like the Apostle Paul, I am a new creature in Christ!

Letting Go

When you begin to run, jog or walk, you will experience what I like to call those zen moments where your mind is clear, your thoughts are few and your feel close to God and the world He created.

When you feel this way, you probably will not worry about what you have to do when you get home, what pressures await at work or care about the unrealistic expectations of others.

Some self-help gurus will say that you are experiencing what is happening "now."

When the running stops, you may also experience what some call runner´s high. Others will call it a strong sense of peace. But in reality, it just a small taste of experiencing God´s unconditional love.

We should let go of things that drag us down. I know it is not easy. But it is senseless to fight a worry battle.

In the book of Romans, this is put into perspective:

"For I am convinced that nothing can ever separate us from his love. Death can't and life can't. The angels won't, and all the powers of hell itself cannot keep God's love away. Our fears for today, our worries about tomorrow, or where we are – high above the sky or in the deepest ocean – nothing will ever be able to separate us from the love of God demonstrated by our Lord Jesus Christ when he died for us." Romans 8:38-39

God has already won the war. Once more, we can appreciate where we are now and enjoy the present moment of peace.

Instead of worry, let us focus on God. Instead of thinking about past hurts and regrets, let us think of this wonderful moment where we are healthy enough to walk or run, breath in fresh air and think about our Savior.

Better yet, why don't you ask Him to walk or run with you.

Running Away From it All

When I was a young girl of 4 or 5 I decided
that was not happy with my parents for some
reason or another and that I was going to
leave home!

I do not remember if I packed a bag or took a
favorite toy, but I do remember leaving the
house. I think it was late afternoon, early
evening.

I remember my parents sitting on the porch as
I stomped off down the street. When I look
back at it, they were probably watching me
with part amusement, part indignation as I
went off in a huff.

Somewhere along my journey down our
street, I became distracted and I was not
watching where I was going. I stepped right
into a sewer grate opening on the sidewalk. It
is a very small opening I guess used to clean
out sewers or water and such. It was broken
and my foot fell into a part of the opening. I
could not move further.

In my new found distress, I called out to my parents who did not quite understand that I was stuck.

But in time, they realized my predicament and finally came to save me from my own mess – even though I was running away from them.

After a few twists of my little foot, my father was able to free my foot from the sewer opening. My white socks were filthy – they were black up to me ankle. And my shoes were a literal mess.

Nonetheless, my daddy picked me up and carried me to the house. While I do not remember what happened next, I am sure that I washed off, hugged, told not to do that again, fed and put to bed.

I don´t remember ever trying to run away again!

When I look back at my toddler-age rebellion, I am reminded of the Biblical story about the prodigal son, who left home to find his own place in life. He wound up spending all of the money (inheritance) his father had given him and was forced to take a job feeding pigs slop. What a vivid picture I have of this!

This prodigal son was also caught with one foot in the sewer. But then he decided to call for help – he got himself together and went back to his father´s house.

When he got home, he was cheerfully greeted by his father, who was going to cook a big meal to celebrate his return.

While home, I am sure that prodigal son got a bath, a good meal and lots of love. Even though he too was rebellious, his father rejoiced when he returned.

How much more our heavenly father rejoices when we return to him after trying to run away. He is always waiting for our return when we stray.

God the Father loves prodigal sons and daughters. He wants the best for us. He is the most loving and merciful parent we could ever have.

I am so glad that when I strayed that he never
let go of me!

Pain

Sometimes when we run, we feel pain in our knees, legs or ankles. We might get side stitches or just feel exhausted. But the trick in being a good athlete is to determine when you should listen to your body´s signals and when you can ignore them.

Sometimes when pain comes, you need to stop – to run more would cause terrible damage to our bodies. Other times we must keep going to fight against fear and laziness disguising itself as pain. We must also guard against spiritual attacks from the enemy who will tell you that you cannot or should not run. We must move past that voice that tells us to just sit down, eat more brownie cake and delay exercise or prayer.

We must also be vigilant when it comes to our past and its negative impact on our daily lives.

We may experience physical, emotional or spiritual pain in our lives and we must determine when we must stop and when we can continue. Our body and spirit will give us signals of what we need to do. We must listen.

If you are running through life taking care of this or that thing for our families and work, yet neglecting your physical pain you are doing yourself purposeful harm. Not going to the doctor to get checked out is dangerous for us, for we are neglecting our bodies. The Bible calls our bodies the temples of God, (please see 1Corinthians 6-19-20).

If we are in terrible emotional and spiritual pain because of loss, death, divorce, work pressures and neglect to take care of this pain them we are damaging our emotional and spiritual health. If we do not find time to talk with our Savior or accept the balance and peace he gives us, then we are damaging ourselves further.

We must heed the danger signs as we see and feel, so that we may avoid the catastrophe of our own making.

I think that sometimes we neglect different aspects of our lives because of fear or because it is easy to do so. When this happens, we can ask God for a heaping of the same courage that he gave Joshua. After the death of Moses God told Joshua to lead Israel in taking the

Promised Land. In my abridged version of the story, Joshua was ordered to walk around a walled city and told that the walls of the city would crumble. Look at the message God gave Joshua before he sent him on the journey:

"Have I not commanded you? Be strong and courageous. Do not be terrified; do not be discouraged, for the Lord your God will be with you wherever you go." Joshua 1:9.

We can walk around the walls in our own life – those that masqueraded as pain and we can see God tear them down.

Yes, sisters, this is possible, because the Bible teaches us that we can do all things in Christ which strengthens us.

So dear sisters, I ask, no I beg you, to act as if you are as courageous as Joshua. Put on some comfortable shoes and begin walking around the walled cities in your life, with hope and thanksgiving and prayer that God will tear down those walls and reduce them to dust.

But take care! Crumbling walls could mean the end of something you consider good in your life to make room for something God believes is superior. It could mean the end of friendships and relationships that are not healthy or leaving a job where your work is not appreciated. It could mean finding a church where you feel more spiritually fed or staying at your church and starting an outreach group in your home to help new members.

Crumbling walls could also mean that you have to face past mistakes and carefully move through the rubble so that you no longer injure yourself.

To me, tumbling walls are scary. It could signify instability, vulnerability to embarrassment. But think of how great it would be if God tore down walls in your life and replaced them with something better, something stronger -- something much more valuable.

I say, let us move out of the Master Builder´s way!

Letting Go of Old Superstitions and Embracing Godly Traditions

My family has a lot of funny traditions and superstitions and some of them rotate around New Year's Day.

The superstitions began when the clock struck midnight.

You see, many of my relatives believe that what you do at midnight is an indication of what you will do all year. So, if you are in your pajamas, giving yourself an avocado facial mask, or snoring in the old recliner chair, this does not bode well for your New Year.

Each year, my family makes an effort to be awake, dressed and ready to embrace the New Year. A glass of bubbly doesn't hurt, either.

Then, there is the tradition/superstition that a man has to be the first person to walk through your door on New Year's Day. A man represented prosperity throughout the year.

However, male relatives did not count in this tradition.

I remember the year when I was a teen and we could not find a man to be our first visitor. We were in a panicked state because we had friends and family who wanted to visit – but they were all embargoed until we could find a "man," to walk through the front door. Luckily, our neighbor Mr. Hatcher saved us from our family crazy.

And then there is the food tradition. In my family it was considered good luck to cook chitterlings. For all of you not familiar with this cuisine, it is spicy, slow simmered, pig intestines. They kind of smell like old gym sneakers when they are cooking, but they taste pretty good. My mom also cooked black-eyed peas and potato salad.

This meal also guaranteed prosperity. But it only seemed to leave most of us with a prosperous amount of gas and indigestion.

I can see now that our family traditions and superstitions were a way to guarantee good times through our own means, rather than relying on the grace and love of God. It was wrong. It's kind of like the Israelites who began worshipping the bronze serpent that Moses had made, rather than God.

In II Kings 18:4 we see that King Hezekiah had this statute destroyed because it became an idol. The following of superstitions also reminds me of I Samuel: Chapter 4, when the Israelites lost a battle against the Phillistines. They thought the loss was because they didn't take the ark of the covenant into battle. So, they had it brought up and they fought again. But 30,000 Israelis died in the battle. While they thought the ark was the key to their victory, they should have instead brought God into the battle with them.

I am grateful that God saved me and my family from our superstitions. But I am also grateful that we have held on to a few traditions. I don't cook chitterlings or black eyed peas. I don't even make resolutions. But, I do enjoy being awake, dressed and being with family when the New Year arrives. And because of God, I am much more aware of the gift of a day, a week, a month and a year. I lean on God for prosperity, whether spiritual or financial and I am grateful for what he gives me.

Happy New Year everyone!

Holiday Havoc

When I was a young girl growing up in Philadelphia, I loved Christmas. I loved getting presents and attending our annual family dinner at my grandmother's house.

But more than that, I also loved the fuss my family made over the holidays:

Christmas decorations had to be brought up from the basement and the house decorated just so;

My mother would go to the Italian market and buy fresh fruits, nuts and chocolates;

I would put up Christmas lights and bake cookies;

And my Grandmother Leona would cook up a literal storm of sweet potato and apple pies, cakes and other sweet treats. And did I mention that she also cooked ham, barbecue pork spare ribs, collard greens, macaroni and cheese, and home-made rolls?

My mouth is watering just thinking about her food!

On Christmas Day we would all gather at my grandmother's house. Someone would always give my Great-Aunt Dot a bit too much brandy and she would always reveal a family secret or two at the family party. We would talk, argue, laugh and reminisce about things past.

Next, we would eat, rest and eat some more. And just when we thought our bellies and hearts were full, my grandmother would unveil her pies.

What can I tell you about my grandmother's pies?

They were awesome. The sweet smell of cinnamon, nutmeg and brown sugar filled the kitchen as she made them. Once they were done, she had to hide them in the house so we did not eat them before the meal. They were so good, that one year a fight nearly broke out when relatives couldn't agree who could take home the leftover pies.

What passion we had for my grandmother's food!

As I got older, I didn't enjoy the holidays so much. I didn't focus on Jesus' birth or being with family. You see, family disagreements and hurts had begun to cloud holiday celebrations. Anger at relatives replaced my joy. Disappointment replaced my laughter. Sometimes I had to work and couldn't fly home to be with the family, other times I didn't want to. Instead of the joy I had for Christmas as a child, I would sometimes find myself battling the holiday blues or full-fledged depression. I am not sure why, but all manner of sad memories can flood you during the holidays.

But when the blues try to visit me now, I can look back and see things more clearly. And what I see cures my sadness. I am grateful for my family. I now laugh at how crazy we behaved over a few pies. I giggle when I think of my Great Aunt Dot and her brandy. I can forgive family trespasses. And I am filled with sadness that my grandmother is no longer here to bake her pies.

What I would give to have another argument over her pies!

I also know that when I feel too much stress that I can take a break and pray to God for help. I can go for a walk or a jog and talk to my Savior during this private time. I know that I will return refreshed and able to handle any holiday issues that may surface.

I also can focus on the most important issue during the holidays and that has more power than any holiday havoc or unpleasant memories: The best holiday gift is not one that we cook, make or give, but the gift that Christ gave us when he died on the cross for us.

Dear sisters, I wish all of you a blessed holiday season filled with love and peace. I pray that your homes will be filled with God's presence. May there be no sadness or holiday blues – but an overabundance of joy. And may everyone in your home get enough pie!

Happy holidays!

Part IV.

Prayers to God

A Prayer of Thanks

Dear God,

Thank you!

Thank you for your love and mercy.

Thank you for my life.

Thank you for blessing my family.

Thank you for all the times you corrected me and purified my heart.

Thank you for legs that can walk, run and move; Thank you for eyes that can be a witness of your beauty, and your creation.

Thank you for strong arms that can hold on to those I love and that can fold up in prayer.

Thank you for loving me unconditionally and never forgetting about me.

Thank you for protecting me and sending angels to fight for me, with me.

Thank you God for not running away from me, especially when there were times I was running away from you. I am glad that you are a faster runner than me. Thanks for reminding me that I belong to you always.

Thank you for walking with me, for talking to me, for quieting my spirit so that I can listen to you.

And, thank you for being my heavenly father.

Amen.

A Prayer to God

Dear Father,

I am not perfect -- I am not even kind of perfect.

But I am glad to be Your daughter.

You are an example of perfection, love and grace.

I do not always act out of love, but you are love.

I have sometimes failed those around me, but you have never failed me. I aspire to do better because you are in my life.

I sometimes try to run from my problems, but you do not run from me.

I have character flaws, but you do not. You love all of me and encourage me to be better, to do better.

I am not perfectly good, but you are truly good.

Your goodness is infinite. There is no counting how many times you forgave me and how much you love me!

Despite all of thing that need to be fixed with me, you thought I was worthy of saving, of being given the wonderful gift of everlasting life.

You are purifying me. You are going to use me for your purpose. You are going to shape me into the Godly woman you intend for me to be.

You have plans for me. You have work for me to accomplish in this life.

I am ready.

I am ready.

Thank you, heavenly father.

I praise Your Heavenly name.

Part V.

Poems

This Silence ...

I hear the crickets as I walk quickly through a meadow. Their soft music captivates even the hurried person. I slow down.

There is serenity here.

I listen and hear more – much more. I hear a sacred silence. God is here, and HE is speaking to me.

I must listen.

I turn. I turn again. Everywhere I turn, I am met with this beauty called silence ...

This silence –

Only the birds and bugs speak here.

Even they are careful about what they say.

I find rest on an old wooden chair.

I sit ... and soak it all inside of me.

Still waiting for God's message

Is it hard for Him to compete with the birds´
songs and crickets´ croons? Am I too
distracted by the beautiful hills and the
intoxicating smell of dew on thin slivers of
grass to hear Him?

A car drives down the winding road that
surrounds this place. It putters about and
momentarily distracts me.

No, I think. He cannot be distracted … and I
believe that he wants me to listen.

The meadow´s dipping, lush hills, the awe of
the grass

Someone gave me a four-leave-clover the
other day.

I put it in my Bible. The Book now rests
under my arm, as I stroll.

I am slowly losing myself here –

In the sounds, sights, smells and stimulation –
My heart is lifted

Is that joy that I feel? The melody of God´s silent music stirs my soul.

I think of my heavenly father and I am glad –

That he showed me this silence, this rest

A butterfly flies from flower to weed. It´s orange color magnified in morning dew. It also needs rest. It does not speak.

A bumblebee passes a nearby chair and does his dance of wonder. He seems to fly in a spiral pattern.

Crickets jump nearby –

There are no worries

This silence – it has freed me from the hassles of work, family.

There are no deadlines or meetings to attend. No pressure. No compromise, no little lies.

This silence, it cannot lie.

Few disappointments await me here –

No boss to make unrealistic demands. There´s no more work. There is only rest in the silence. I feel warmth and no fear

A cool wind blows by

It too surrounds me – in God´s love

I look at the aqua sky – with white puffs and honey streamers. The clouds have lost its battle with the sun

My heart has been warmed.

I think of my Savior, when He died on the cross. He died for my sins – yet He still loves me.

I wait. I see. I hear. I know.

I await a message from God. There has been nothing said here.

I take a deep breath; He calls me by my name.

"Little one, my child, little one – Be still and know that I Am the Lord thy God. I have

created this silence for all to enjoy," I feel
Him say.

I feel a warm breeze flowing through the air,
just touching my skin.

I stand ...

I watch ...

I share ... This silence and know that my God
is near.

The Great – Is Near

God is the Great I Am,
But my ignorance prevents me from knowing
Him.

I read His heavenly word and I pray often.
I talk to others about His grace. But still, he is
a mystery. And I was never good at puzzles or
´who done it,´ books.

One day, I decided to change the way I pray –
to stop asking for things and to simply talk to
Him – to tell God about my day – everyday,
      My mistakes,
      My sins,
      My disappointments,
      My regrets,
      My dreams.

I tell Him about my past, my struggles. I ask
for forgiveness. I beg him to heal my wounds.

Sometimes I didn´t always get what I needed.
Sometimes there was no support for my
dreams.

I still feel the eternal pain of abuse, the marks of violence. There is such hopelessness inside me.

"Free me from this darkness," I beg Him.
Is he listening? I am not sure.
Again and again I pray to Him – The Great I Am, who is always near.
I am so haunted by my past – lots of lost opportunities and blatant disregard for His truth.

Does He listen to my prayers?
I know he does, but I do not feel certain. But I talk to Him anyway.
I tell him of the days when I was hungry – the days when money and food didn´t stretch to the end of the month.

I am still hungry. But now, I am hungry for God´s truth – the truth that will cleanse me. But my past blurs my vision and causes such pain.

"Free me from this depression," I beg.
Is he listening? I wonder again. I keep talking.

I remind God of His promises to me – that he will never leave or forsake me.

How do I know that he is even there?

I tell God everything. I hope that maybe he might hear a few words if not all of them.

If he has time to hear –

Exhausted, I begin telling God how I was taunted as a child. I was teased because I wore hand-me-downs. I was such a nervous character that I sometimes peed my pants. I developed a rash from it. The scars still adorn my inner thighs, like lace stencils.

"Are you listening to me?" I ask.

"You promised to watch over me," I said. I am angry now – even demanding.

"Are you even there?"

Nothing … was the reply.

Is it my ignorance that prevents me from knowing Him? Am I deaf to his words and kindness or are my deeds beyond even God´s precious grace?

"I am so angry that I want to shake my fists at you," I yell, looking up at my moldy bedroom ceiling. "But I know what that would mean. It would mean that I could be cut off from you – and that is not what I want.

God where are you? By now I am screaming.
I don´t want my neighbors to think that I am
crazy --perhaps it´s too late for that. Momma
once told me that insanity ran on both sides
of our family.

Salty tears ran down my face. Even they have
a bitter taste.
"I don´t know you. But I know that you have
got to be there. You have to hear me. I know
you heard me – at least part of what I had to
say."
"You say in the Bible that you will never leave
me."
"You say seek and I will find. Then, why can´t
I find you God? Isa this some sort of game? I
don´t play games well."
Are you just too busy to listen or do you have
more important things going on up there?
"I know the world and this galaxy are large. I
know the people on earth are troubled. There
is great pain and no one seems to really care
about each other."
But can´t God give me some time?
Just tell me a good time to talk with you, so I
will have your full attention.

My tears are now blinding me – well it´s really my tears mixing with my eye-liner. The pain is a bit unbearable. My nose is stopped up.

I feel so rejected by God. I also feel rejected by all the people in the world. I have all the material I need to build a better person and a better life.
I am not hungry. I have a refrigerator filled with fresh fruits, vegetables and lean cuts of meat. I have money to travel and spend. I have a nice home. Even my bedroom is not too bad.
I am sitting on my floor, surrounded by big pillows.

But things don´t matter much. Especially if you feel cut off from God. "Unless you talk to me, nothing else seems to matter," I shout.
I don´t remember all of what I said to God. I just know that my throat was hoarse when I got done. I had had it with this God, who was supposed to be near and a religion where I was supposed to be perfect. I thought I was doing right, after doing so much wrong.
"Little one," God interrupts my agony.
"I AM,"''
"What Lord?" I ask. "I AM."

"I AM … Here … with You."

"You talk to me often," I can feel him say.

"But you do not listen. How can I speak to you child if you cannot hear Me over your own words."

"I AM … Here … Always."

Shock isn´t even part of what I feel. I hear HIM. I hear God and He is talking to me. I heard what He said!

Maybe He really does love me! I mean something to Him. Therefore, I must mean something to Him!"

That day, I listened to God. He said many things. He said that nothing could ever separate me from His love.

For hours, I sat and listened – something I have rarely done not only with God, but with all things that speak in life – conscience, love, nature, desire, man.

My ignorance has been transformed by Him, into knowledge.

I know the Great I AM is near and hears me. I know,

He is there and if I want to know what He thinks and what He plans for me,

All is have to do is ask, and LISTEN!

Part VI.

An important first step for your journey

Confession of Faith

If you do not know Christ, I invite you to accept him into your heart as your Lord and Savior from sin.

To become a Christian, ask God to come into your heart and life. You can confess this Bible verse, as I did when missionaries visited my neighborhood. You can replace the "your" with "my" and "I":

(I) *"... Confess with your mouth, Jesus is Lord, and believe in your heart that God raised him from the dead, you will be saved." Romans 10:9.*

Welcome to the family dear sister!

You may also take this time to talk to God about what is on your heart. He loves to listen!

I became a Christian on _____

I invite you to visit a local church and find a church home. Also, talk to your new pastor about officially joining the church and being baptized. Remember that God loves you and he will never leave you or give up on you!

If you are already a Christian and have strayed away, God is inviting you to return. Pray now to rededicate yourself to him. He loves you and will accept you as you are.

I rededicated myself to Christ on _____

Remember sister that it is good for you to go to church and surround yourself with believers who can help you grow in your faith.

If you are a long-time Christian, I encourage you to mentor other women – if you don´t do this already. You could start a Christian running group or have weekly prayer walks with other women. If you prefer to exercise alone, you can meet with friends at your house or a local restaurant for weekly talks, prayers and good eats.

It is good to exercise our body so that we can be healthy and able to answer God´s call on our lives!

May we all continue to run for our lives … with God!

For group Discussion

1. After reading this devotional, what are some of your thoughts about your faith walk?

2. Have you ever stumbled? What were the keys to getting back up and moving along His path?

3. What were your stumbling blocks and how have they been removed?

4. How can you take this message in a non-judgmental way to others who are struggling to find their way?

5. How has your faith strengthened you in times of crisis? And if you did not turn to your faith in troubling times, how can you equip yourself to do so when troubles come?

6. If you have young daughters, do you walk with them? And if so, can you share your faith walk with them?

7. Do you pray when you walk or run? It can be helpful to set aside some time of your physical exercise for prayer.

8. Could you commit to doing a weekly faith walk alone, of with friends so that you all may pray together?

9. Use this portion of the devotional to write down some of your thoughts and feelings about "running for your life."

_____
_____

10. What else would you like to share with the group?

About the Author: Richelle Clark has worked as a journalist and or educator in Germany, Honduras and the United States. She has also lived in other countries, including Portugal and Brazil.

Clark taught at the Missouri School of Journalism and has had a love affair with words since she was a child. She continues to walk or run along the Lisbon Coast and hopes that you will continue to run for your life.

To help you on your journey, she is also developing a spiritual marathon for all to follow. For more information, check out the website www.runforyourlife.mobi in 2012.

www.ingramcontent.com/pod-product-compliance
Lightning Source LLC
Chambersburg PA
CBHW071822020426
42331CB00007B/1587